Whispers

A Collection of Poems

Whispers

Millicent Pryce

Whispers
A Collection of Poems

Copyright ©2015 by Millicent Pryce

ISBN 978-976-95859-0-4
Illustrator: Nicholas Barrett

Acknowledgements

"Commit thy way unto the Lord; trust also in him; and he shall bring it to pass."

Sometimes I read my poetry and wonder if it is I who actually wrote them. On my own, I don't consider myself capable of doing anything so I thank God for first giving me the potential to do so much then putting the right people in my life to help me to unearth my talents and skills.

I am grateful to my immediate family, the Denbigh High School family, my lecturers, friends, supporters and acquaintances for inspiring, teaching, supporting, guiding and tolerating me on my journey to having this accomplishment.

Also, I appreciate the many people who will take time to read my poems and share in my love for the many faces of life.

May your thirst for words be quenched from this glass of my mind!

Cheers!!

Foreword

Whispers…

It is amazing how much time we spend listening to other people complain about life and criticize people; yet we spend so little listening to our own thoughts about this and that. Fear might just be the culprit, maybe the words are just too harsh or it could simply be the reason of ignorance that causes us to do it. So we drown our thoughts with technology, turn the music up loud, keep busy then we go to sleep.

You know, there is something graceful and soothing about silence. It speaks to me. I have no doubt it speaks to pretty much everyone – except that only some listen. It comes as a whisper; unhurried, calm, pensive, compassionate and so many things. You don't have to be alone to hear it; the peace in your head is enough.

Silence is what helps me to write…I avail myself to it. Whether alone or in company, I am conscious of who I am and I tune in to life; its ups and downs and the people around me. It is not enough to just exist. One must truly live and care about the living in order to appreciate the words which define them.

This anthology is a combination of heart and mind…careless whispers tossed about a listening soul.

What is your mind trying to tell you?

Dedication

This book is dedicated to my mother, Joan Rowe, who has devoted her life to my education, growth and development and my sister Sonia Pryce Ramsay whose love and support are a constant source of encouragement. I love you both and I will be forever grateful.

... With unsung melodies

The air ripples in a silent hum,

Whispering to hearts that listen,

And to minds that feel...

Whispers...

The first sigh of the morning…
Till the last sweat of the evening
Is punctuated by careless whispers –
Lost to unseeing eyes
Sheltered by listening ears
And captured by open hearts…

Themes n titles

Heaven and Earth

Societal Hiccups

Between the Lines

Affairs of the Heart

Affairs of the Heart

Streams of Consciousness

Heaven and Earth

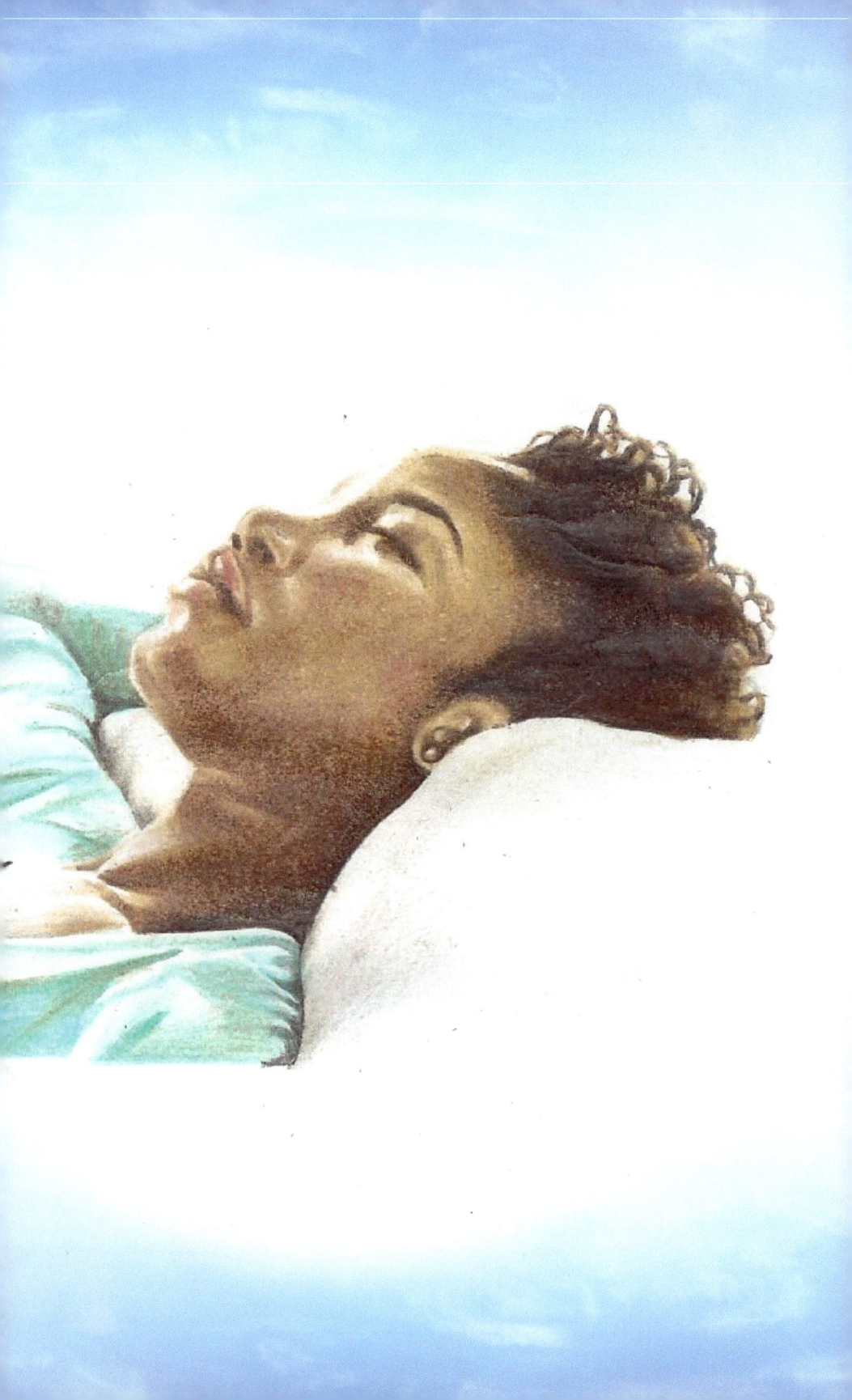

Day's Rest

When day goes to sleep
under its thick dark blanket
stars come out to peep below the colorless sky.
With dim winking lights
They stare with all their might
At dozing lives –
Cuddled in the embrace of the night.

In its chilly ambience
Is spared not a trace of blue
And the perky moon gives all but a clue.
In its many dreams can be found me and you,
A tired little bundle –
Unconscious in its dew.

Musing Valleys

O mountains so majestic and tall
How I the valleys muse beside your great giant wall,
Ever so green, ever so high;
I wish I too could be close to the light.
Such great wonders your eyes are privileged to see,
My heart yearns for the day when on your shoulders
you volunteer to hold me,
O what splendor! O what bliss!
To be ever so strong, ever so sure, always a force
to be reckoned with.
Dear lofty, pristine mother of plains and I;
My soul longs for the nature to grow as should a child
with dreams and questions of 'why'
yes what joy, what emancipation it would be
if for a change I could be you and you be me
have you any wonder of what it's like to be beneath –
far far below mighty clouds, travelling trees and at your feet?
Look down on me again ye bearer of awe and pride
See how my neck angles backward to stare at your side
Consider your blessings and hope not to fall
while I the valleys pray for height and continue to muse beside
your great giant wall.

The Broken Flight

In awe, I sat and watched as it took flight,
Its delicate yet reliable wings
Took it spiralling through the midday air
Willing it to safety from the gun man's stare –
For it was its season of the year.
I heard the shots;
The cries of others as they drop.
But, for the safety of this one was all I cared
Its tiny wings hadn't taken it far enough still,
And then;
Another shot came…
I heard an haunting scream –
My feet took me running to it,
My hands reached out to catch it,
And my eyes;
They slowly dive with its broken flight
And while its whimpers lingered on the afternoons' sleeve
I cried.
Even after there was nothing.

Daylight

When night awakes from its long deep slumber,
It retires from its black pajamas
To become dressed in the silky cloak of daylight
Like a frantic child it scurries out to drink of flowers dew
Then not long afterwards stir me awake
Just so I may hurry to come out and see you
With insight that for me beautiful smiles and warm friendliness
awaits;
It lingers still…
Until the sky is no longer blue.

On the Rails

Innocence sat in the lap of an elderly rail,
Bubbling with laughter and tales and secrets
Untraded with their mothers or fathers
For fear of the beatings of belts as wheels are to the rails –
Time has caught them there on countless occasions –
Like when Tinkerbell died and funeral arrangements
had to be made and the time when Frisky's pups
had to be christened,
they are like pure white Lilies – those two
Running wild on the wrinkled boards with the wind
at their tails and freedom floating through their hair
Their squeals of joy touch the heavens like the choral symphony
of a thousand angels
and their memories on the rails are like endless years of diamonds
glowing in a dark abyss
O, to feel their thrill as tiny feet propel them to unseen horizons
Is to see the rails
To touch the thought of it and hear the wheels of an unseen train
Listen to the silent rumble which takes with it the fulfilled wishes of
waiting eyes
Whose dreams lay scattered on the rails.

Societal Hiccups

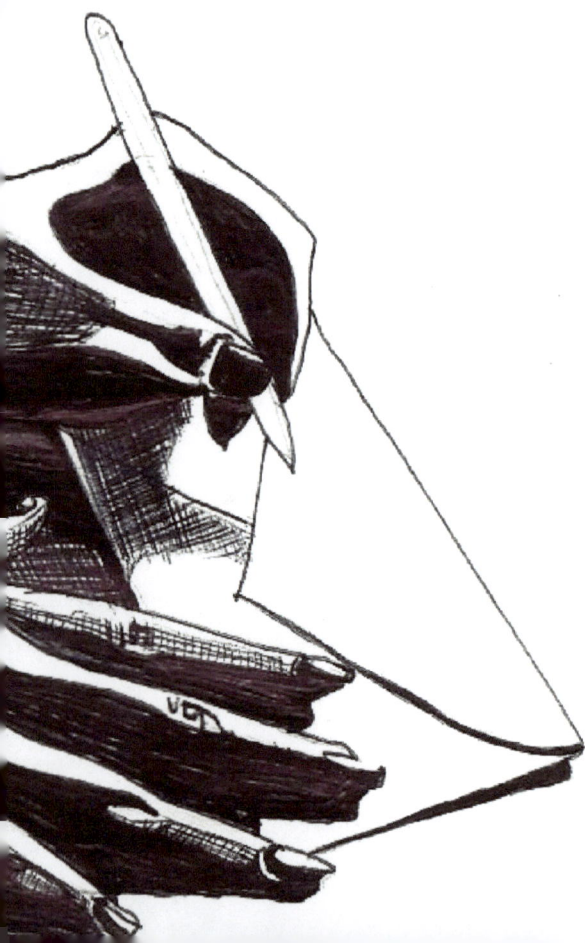

To my dear Aunt Jenny with Love

Aunty, I've found someone – finally!
As lie as honesty and as sure as
tomorrow is how I describe this one,
yes Aunty is true! 'im different different
not one minute no past an dis man don't ask mi
if mi hungry!
('im seh 'im waan 'phat' mi up!)
Excuse my language aunty-it's just that this man
Has excited me in the most excitable way-
And oh-it's a man that I'm talking about-
Please remember that I am eighteen as of the day before
Yesterday and the other day before that
So don't think you can go complain to mommy or daddy
An' all a unnu come try stop mi.
He took me to this gigantic hotel yesterday, it is superbly beautiful-
Am writing you from one of the rooms right now-you ought to spend
At least a weekend in these places-
Or have you been doing so with uncle George in secret?
I was probably too young to realize anyway-

Mommy and daddy are ok and so too are
Kerry and Shaun.
Say hi to Uncle George for me
And can I ask you a tiny favor Aunty Jenny please...
Could you bring me one of those nice lingerie that are sold
over there?
I've seen them being advertised on TV
Thanks a whole lot in a dvance!

From your niece
With lots of love!!!

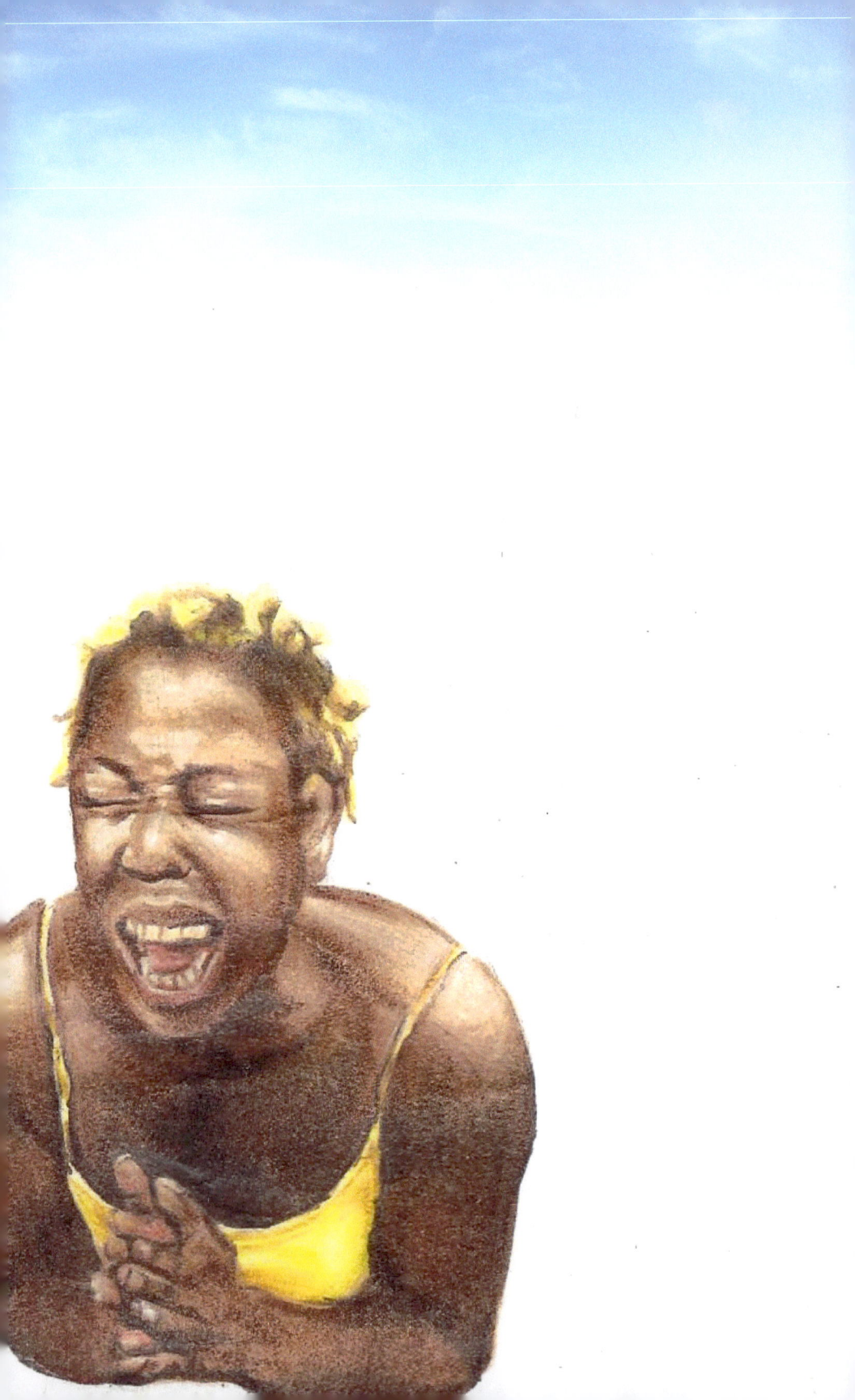

A Cry for Help

Extricate this monster that bellows from my roof,
Silence its sneers so that in my own soul I can have some peace,
Put a rope around its neck,
Kill it if you will; I won't open my doors to sympathy!
Get rid of it! Shoot it with your gun,
Trample it under your feet,
Please….
Is anyone hearing me?
Release me from the chains of my mentality,
I want some time to be alone with me.
Hush now…hush…I didn't mean to sound rude,
Just bear with me while I try to regain my sanity…

You…
Open your ears to the scream of my pleas,
Swallow that thought that pulls back your hand,
Help me…please…
Don't do it again…don't!
Please don't turn and run away,
The nail he drives through my mind kills my life,
Slowly…but surely it does,
I beg you to stay, help me to convince myself of another's care,
Put your hands upon my head,
Let them sleep gently there until this monster is no longer there,
Hush now…hush…I didn't mean to sound rude,
Just bear with me while I try to regain my sanity.

Saddened Child

Our father,
Whose family he has forsaken
Pity is his name
Too bad things didn't remain the same
Now he'll have to take the blame

Many a night I cry
It is may as well I just die
What wouldn't I give?
If only I could change my parents' plight

Why?
My mother you beat
There were other ways
Couldn't you see it?
No need to have placed her at your feet
She didn't cheat,
Did you have to do it?

I pitied the do or
It sobbed too am sure
Watching the departures of one from four
Worsening the situation even more
He didn't seem to care one bit
Tell us something dad,
Where did your love go?
The one you expected us to face survival with –

Frustration seeps in
Why should anyone live like this?
It is a sin
Didn't you think we'd detect your lies?
Put an end to my 'whys'
My frustration needs translation

We,
Your children were to be the future
Now
To others lives we'll be a torture
Because of your attitude we are so depressed
Anger and disappointment
We have failed to suppress
In school
We fail to progress
Missing all the juices of sweet success

Whose fault it was
I ache to repeat
Mom wasn't perfect
But
Neither were you dad
Why;
This imperfection made us all very sad
Without divorce I'd have been one happy lad.

Why did you do it

Pull me into your arms and caress my cheeks with the filthy
Palms of your hand…
Breathe the stale air of your polluted mouth in my innocent face…
Glide those illegal hands up and down the contours of my small
body…
Reveal and revel in my unripe-repulsed-trembling-cold-burning
temple…
Our flesh

How can you?
Day after day grind your hip against mine like…like – (lovers!)
Whisper such bitter sweet lullabies to me in my own bed,
Then like a babe cuddle with Mom in the dead of the night

Love me again Daddy…
just not in that way
PLEASE!
I want to love you too
In exactly the way little girls
should love their fathers…

Mom! Moooomm?
Why can't you hear me?
HELP!
(oh please don't drown in the sea of my
tears before you hear my pain…)
Daddy DON'T touch me there!
MOM?

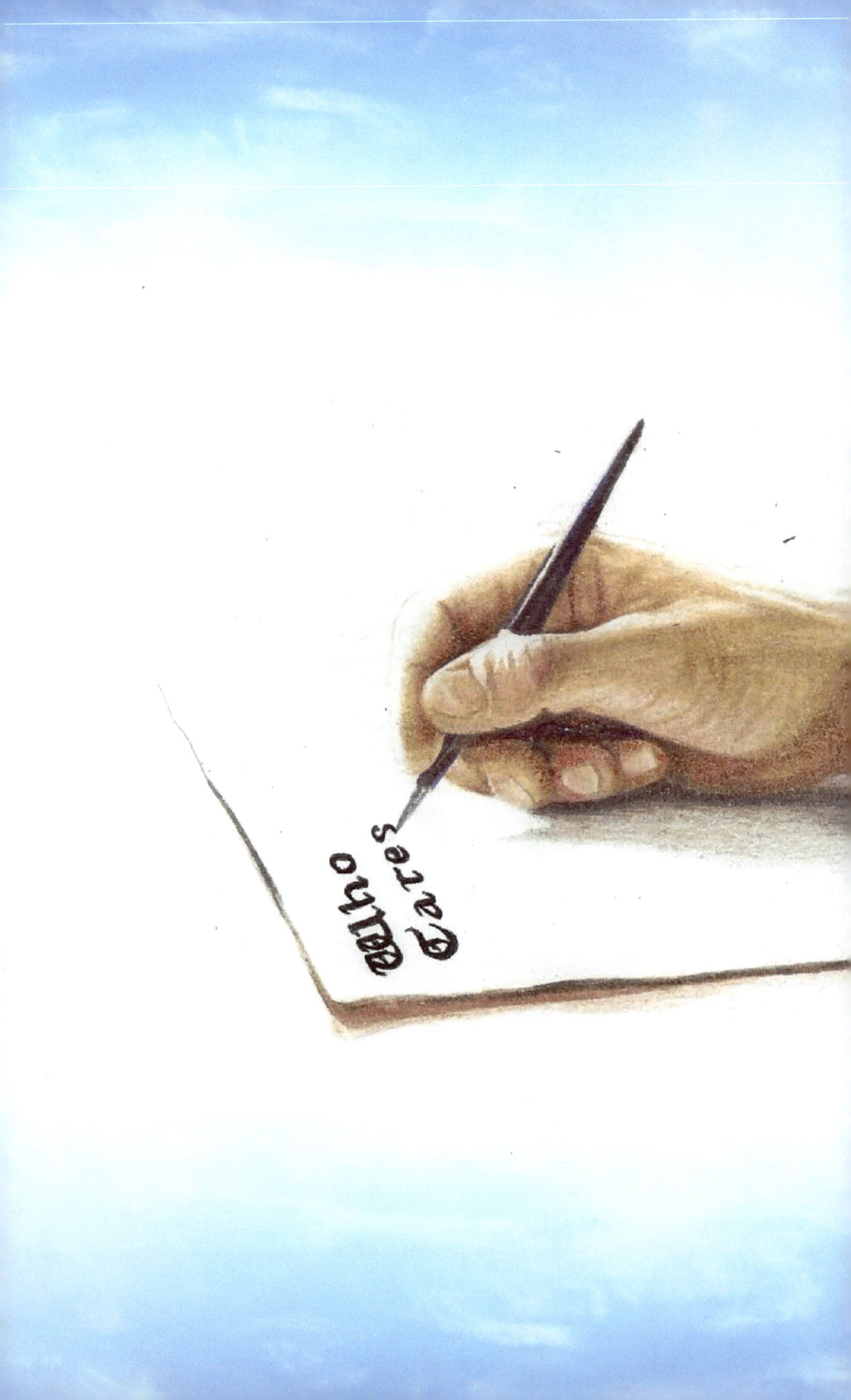
Who cares

Who cares

About a soul lost in a world void of feeling?
empty and broken by venomous words and lack in time -
the giver and taker of all things.
Who cares
About a life lived meaninglessly in toil, smile and
pretentious joy?
trampeled, unappreciated, unloved - depressors of
human spirit.
Who cares
If a heart dies from the aches of betrayal, hunger
for love and thirst for pure emotions that flow from
springs of sincerity and oneness?
who cares...
about a soul that is lost,
about a life that is lived meaninglessly,
about a heart that is dying,
do you?

Between the Lines

Just the Opposite

I hate it when the wind caresses my skin,
Because it takes away the sweat of the sun and makes me
feel comfortable and at peace.
Why do the birds sing so sweetly even though their homes are being
destroyed?
I find it disgusting and unbearable;
How I wish winter would come and beckon them away.
Can't the clouds be a darker shade of blue or maybe pink?
I don't think I like it the way it is,
It is too ugly and dull.

I think flowers would smell better if they didn't wear any perfume;
Bright colorful petals make them too fragile to look at;
maybe it would have been better if they were made with cement and
steel.
The sea would look so much better if it was yellow and if its waves
stood still;
Imagine how comforting the sand would feel if it was as hard as rocks.
Nothing could be more appealing than water that is dry.

Life could be lived so much easier if it was dead all together,
No smiling faces to dampen its days and no humour to make it cry.
With no sun, it would be brighter
And without forever it would still be existent.

I don't like the way everything is,
Things would be so much better if they were just
the opposite of everything I say.

The Reunion

In a moment of deja-vu they look at each other –
One plainly white the other black, white and pondering
The air between them crackles with the air of forgotten familiarity
But plainly white has nothing to say and black white and pondering
Has much but knows not where to start.

Like two old couple who have long grown out of love –
And soft gentle words to stain the heart of the other;
They pose in a trance of unspoken tension,
Until a reeling mind spit a word then two unto plainly white's sleeve
Two words stretch as birthmarks across the white belly
And there is no stop until plainly white resembles yesterday's eve

As the coil unwind; the air shifts, simmers and settles
Into the comfort of lifelong friends with secrets to trade and scars to
unveil
No longer is the yearlong silence a binding shackle
As with one word…then two – came the reunion.

Where my thoughts Rest

Snow white, trapped between thin borders of blood,
Lays face down on the smooth plane of my desk;
patiently awaiting the slashes of my pen and the weight of my words.
Though already wounded by thin blue lines running horizontally
along her belly,
She accepts my feelings gracefully and treasures them for as long as she
is allowed,
Never does she refuse my thought's right to rest;
Les' she be disturbed by a passing wind or an unintended sweep.

Between the lines of her wounded tummy she permits my voice,
With a promise to always reflect them given my eyes desire to see.
She sometimes echo my thoughts to others but hardly do I hold it
against her,
for I should know that without concealing her wounds she is sure to
bleed.
When however, I am in doubt of her discretion,
I rip her to tiny pieces so that nobody else is permitted to see,
sentences that should be read, only by me.

Snow white, trapped between thin borders of blood,
Lays face down on the smooth plane of my desk;
Stained by the many tales I had to tell,
and more educated than she had ever been.
Though I manipulate and sometimes abuse the extent of her
generosity;
She still makes space for me in her open wounds,
And for that I love her.
I love her for the facilitation she makes for my mind's expression;
the place where my thoughts rest.

Empty

Like a child's eyes, after the last tear of a tantrum had been spilt,
is a noisy barrel, lost to the essence and beauty of silence
the belly of a barren woman makes no difference –
for it defines an absence of which hearts are yet to grow fonder.
Empty
Life, leaving no correction to the definition of vacuum,
Gives a mind such talent as to paint a space – capturing effortlessly,
The face of Nothing.
And through it all a heart pulses, dripping the last of its tap into
a docile soul to become the last breath of a lung
Empty
Like me, after the last parcel of emotions have been trampled,
is a dried lake, stripped naked by the coldness of a drought,
a toppled bottle of syrup left open is much the same –
for it no longer holds that which made it sweet.

Skin Deep

Roses blossom in the sanctuary of my soul
Adorn the sidewalks and scent the cold.
Hide the weeds, shun the heat
Welcome the sun for all to see.
Hurry along the little ones-
Fear their disturbance of Hummingbird songs.

Rivers run deep in the well of my heart,
They sing the songs of a musician's harp.
Think of how they sway their hips around a stone,
like noisy emotions confused by the unknown.
Imagine the depths of their cool façade,
Bring the thought of caution as your aid.

Illuminated daylight, mysterious night…
Reveal my secrets, hide your face.
Test my endurance with consuming plights,
Withdraw your hope
Leave me to find my own.

Rooted trees, swaying branches-
Stand your ground, shed the leaves,
Count me among your ripening fruits,
Hold me by the stem and preserve my seeds.

Maddening love murderous hate,
Rent my life, evict my heart,
Saturate me with the joys of fate.

Perfect order detangled from chaos,
For you my life is in agonizing lust.

Flesh beneath skin, skin above flesh-
Show your true colours for the world to see-

Mysterious daylight, illuminated night
I've conquered your challenges
So here I am now,
With nothing to hide.

Affairs of the Heart

My Love

With the passing of time; you are all I see,
You captivated my thoughts and willingly gave your love to me.
In my dreams you will always be,
loving me with a love that goes very deep.

Like a knight you hold my heart,
Guarding my emotions for all its worth,
Without your love, a genuine one,
I'd be lost to the dirt
Finding no happiness regardless of how I might search.
Take me in your arms,
Quench my new found love of its prolonged thirst.

My love for you is like an everlasting flame;
It burns with a fire that can't be tamed,
The intensity of its heat can't be named
And until the end of time
I will love you just the same.

Distant Nearness

I think I love you but I still feel alone,
Many times I wish you were here
instead of being over the phone.
I understand our situation but I can't help but to want you near,
There are so many sides to us;
So much that we need to share.
How do you feel being so far away?
Do you have someone else giving you my 'special care'?
I wouldn't like that.
You say you love me; come here,
Come prove it to me if you dare.

I feel empty.
My hands…, my heart…and my love;
They reach out for you, but you are too far away,
The seas are too wide to cross;
And the mountains simply won't move,
How can I reach you?
Please; don't suggest that I call;
I've trod that road before,
It does nothing for my wounded heart.
Your declaration of love means a lot for sure,
But I'd love even more your demonstration of the art.

Secret Affair

Let us meet by the lake of discretion,
to consummate our love,
Come with me and we'll ride the waves of
pleasure,
dance to the rhythm of ecstasy
and under the starlit sky feast in the boat
of intimacy.
Tell no one of our furtive plan…
For we are not in want of wagging tongues
or inquisitive disturbances.

Come when the moon is set far into the sky
and daylight is completely immersed in the thickness
of its dark blanket.
If you will be missed…give her a hug and promise to
Only be away for a while
(I can bear the scent of her perfume but not the taste of her
on you.)
Trod softly so the neighbors won't hear…
But don't be too long for I too shall be missed when
Time betrays our moment of bliss.

Touch my senses with the magical whisper of your lips,
Ache with the need for my feathery caresses
And fill me with the thunder of your storm…
So that both of us being wet can quench each other's thirst
Then retire to our individual shores
satisfied with our conquest of a mighty romance.

Kiss me just once again and lets go our way
For by now we must be sought by those awaiting
us at home.

Undo this love

I try to see us from every angle
And the only vision clear is me in a love triangle
How can I destroy a perfect thing
When in the end there is nothing for me to win…?

If you are her Romeo and she your Juliet
Just what am I to you…
Your 'not-sure-yet?'
I want no part of this love indigestion
So my suggestion…
Let's undo this love.

Undo your tender midnight kisses
And stop those reminiscent speeches
Of what we had and can become,
For I can see through all the illusions,
though I am still young.

We can still impregnate our impenetrable distance
With multiple calls multiple times per day
But know that in no way and by no chance
Am I going to be fooled by anything you say.

Love is such a rare lesson learnt
But like eraser to paper I will undo that typographical error
And save myself the charred remains of a heart badly burnt
By dread, regret and sorrow
For a tangled love affair that never became undone.

The Quarrel

The words,
As bitter as a pill they came
And just so, I swallowed them.
In their harsh bitterness
I heard the anguish
The contempt
I even saw and felt the pain in them
What if I had just told the truth?
Maybe, just maybe
It would have merited softer words –
And so they continue coming,
The words
But, by now I have become overdosed
And the tears emptied,
Drowning the others, maybe much worst.

Your Pain

I hear it in your voice
And my heart heaves with sorrow;
I watch it flicker in your eyes and
Mine swim with comprehension
It manifest itself in the trembling of your hands
And I ache to offer you a touch
So much of your pain engulfs me that now I
Must enfold you into the comfort of an embrace –
Let our tears fall together
Empty the words that constrict your heart,
And know that they bind mine too;
They arrest the depths of my emotions because from
My imaginings,
I too am withered by your distress
And though I take this much of what isn't duly mine
It is sad but true that in the end…
It will all still be your pain.

If

If words could close the distance between us,
there is nothing that I would leave unsaid.
For every second, I would utter a word
maybe sing a few
cause that way it takes less time to be closer to you.

If words were a ship, maybe a plane,
no ticket or fair could hinder my being next to you
If they were a car or maybe a train
I wouldn't have to worry about them running out of fuel
on the road to be with you.

If words had the same effect as an action,
I would use them to do everything;
like showing you how much I care...
and so many other things.

If........,
If words could replace the time that
we need to understand each other;
to earn the mutual respect that is
needed for a relationship to strive,
there is nothing that I wouldn't do to gather
as much as I can,
that I might use them to make a watch,
maybe a clock....,
and that way I would have perfect control of the
time that is needed to achieve that...,
That way the time would be less....,

If words could...,
If words were...,
If words had...,
if...

Mr. Valentine

Dear Mr. Valentine:
I want chocolate, cake, ice cream, flowers and love when you come,
Roses to be exact…deep deep red and crystal white ones.
I love my chocolate the shade of your skin…rich and creamy
And my ice cream, the flavor of your lips-
Heavenly soft, wistfully sweet and blissfully sensual.

The butterflies of my heart are fluttering now…
Joy has laid a nest in my soul and anticipation a trail of
seduction in my mind.
Just how far have you reached my dear valentine?
I hope you know that even for your innocent delay-
You'll be the victim of my wicked love –
Embers in my candle trays…petals on the floor…on my bed…secret
pleasures in my head and you in my web-

Patience eludes me but wait I must for your arrival
Comforted by the faith that time is a punctual train
and even as the gentle fingers of a loitering breeze caress my skin…
I will be thinking of you…wanting you…and waiting for your arrival.

A Place in my Heart

Traces of your laughter still linger in my mind,
It rings softly, crystal clear
Clear as the bright blue skies that watched as we stood
Side by side talking and laughing about nothing at all,
Your eyes still sparkle when they come to visit my mind
And each time they do, my heart leaps and claps and dance
I loved my love for your love to have had me and you in our
Company,
Being with you was hardly ever a dull moment,
Your presence to me was like Christmas
Jolly, festive, fun and not long enough –
I wish now that I could crawl on the hands of time to recapture
Those blissful moments,
My hands want to touch and embrace you again –
If all I can now have of you are memories of yesterday,
I will never cease wishing you back into my tomorrows
I wish so badly that I could touch your voice as it echoes in my head,
I wish ever so earnestly that I could feel your smile touching
my lips as it once did,
I wish on my every breath that I could still breathe your every thought
I wish and I wish and I wish that you were still here with me
Without 'u' my soul is incomplete
If 'u' were not in my thoughts they would all be meaningless -
There are so many things that I am not without you
But as long as forever you will always be a place in my heart.

Your Laughter

Is your laughter like rustling leaves in scurrying breeze
Or may I liken it to the symphony of a vivacious band?
Thoughts of how it causes your belly to dance make me smile
I wonder too if tears spill from your eyes as you stagger from side to
side
Enraptured by the humour of the moment –
A time you'll never have again; the experience of now;
I wish I was there to laugh with you,
To cling to you so that we stagger together
And like this breath capture the moment forever.
Since I am here – and you there
Laugh.
I will smile,
Happy that life is kind to you amidst its drudgery and despair
and generous to me with the means for this moment to share.

Streams of
Consciousness

Lifetime

A usual and consistent routine;
life gets dressed in its numerous garments and
goes out hand in hand with time to explore.
On their explorations they came across burdened hopeless
people; tossed and turned in the suffocating embrace of dark tunnels,
looking at them with deep contemplation; life became moved with
compassion,
'Something must be done for these people.' It whispered to time,
Touched by the tear in life's voice, time said; 'Don't worry; I will take
care of them for you.'
'But time, you are so patient and independent, can't you see they are
about to
give up on me, something must be done now.'
All humble and wise, time said nothing but allowed life to do as it will
for the people,
From its giant bag of opportunities, life took out second chances for
people who have failed in pursued dreams and for others who never
had any,
thrilled from observing their reactions, life stood aside and watch
to see what the once hopeless people would now do with their
opportunities,
while some saw the new light that was shed on their lives, others were
buried too deep in self pity and hopelessness to make good of it,
Time took a deep breath in anticipation of life's disappointment,
It was not long before some of the people who realize what they have
received close the door of opportunity that was opened for them,
Discouraged, confused and overdosed with doubt; they spat in life's
face,

A knot of distress tied in life's stomach and time placed a hand around its shoulders while wiping tears with a free hand,
'Oh time, just what more can I possibly do to make them accept and appreciate me for what I am, I've done everything I can possibly do.'
Life wept.
Patiently, Time looked at life and said; 'Don't worry; I will take care of them for you.'

Life

Search

A Conversation with Life

Life, do you have a minute?
I was wondering if maybe we could sit down and talk,
I am really hoping you won't mind.
There are some things that I want to ask you about,
How do you feel being exhaled from so many different souls?
Do you ever wish that you were never born?
I mean; with people being so consistently brutal to you,
How do you feel?

Child; I've cried rivers and seas,
But my tears have become an instrument for leisure,
I really don't mind though, as long as the smile of my sun I
continuously
see,
I've broken a couple of hearts too you know, did them well
I doubt they learn as much from their broken feet
Walk with me my child, this journey will show you what my words
can't tell…

As the days come and go, I sit and look and listen,
To the insults…the criticisms…the compliments…the justice and the
injustices
Thrown in your face, most times without a care or even second
thought;
And you are saying it really doesn't matter?
How? I know I've done you some wrongs, maybe many,
I find it hard to forgive me sometimes, yet you find it easy to forgive
so many,
How?

(Soft laughter), I am what I am child;
A heart meant to be broken and repaired,
T''is true many try to make me feel inferior,
Are unsatisfied with my being;
The wise see it best to accept me for what I am,
I've had fair treatment from others,
And so what if some try and do succeed at wiping me from the face of
the earth;
I've had it all child; and nothing ever changes,
Cause I am what I am
A heart meant to be broken and repaired.

Death

Life is so short;
You never know when it might end,
Ensure to cherish in your heart
Every moment shared with family and friends,
Never take anything for granted
Because you might never see them again.

Death is breathtaking and has no appeal;
When it knocks at your door
Many are the emotions that you feel
From such a tragedy there is no detour;
The emptiness it brings is like a scar not even time can heal
And grief, regret and disbelief are wounds you are left to endure.

Nothing is as indifferent as death;
The void left by its robbery is one one can never forget
For though it takes of the lives we love
The memories they've left imprinted on our hearts
Are too deep to dissect,
And so it leaves us that bit of treasure,
A trace of their existence – much to its regret.

A lesson not Learnt

Don't fall for a smile,
Please…neither for the whispers of flowery words.
Their bruises are nasty
and after months of nursing the wounds they inflict;
The point of impact will still be sore ---
A lifetime of experiences ought to let me know.

Tell your mind to not conceive the thought that everyone
Mean you well…
Less you dine naively with the relatives and friends of deceit;
Play into their traps and be made a clown.
Their minds are as clean as a criminal's record-
and their tongues – the finest of wines.
The tools of their trade are seasoned for the subtle purging of your
blood-
Be warned or kneel to a point of rest beneath vines.

Have you weighed the sincerity of their intentions?
And what of the bars cleverly set about your mentality for your 'best'
interest?
Much is left to be questioned but is not for me to mention,
Open your eyes – free your mind and it will show you the rest…
Of bleached darkness…stones left unturned---
Pay attention or be the victim of a lesson not learnt.

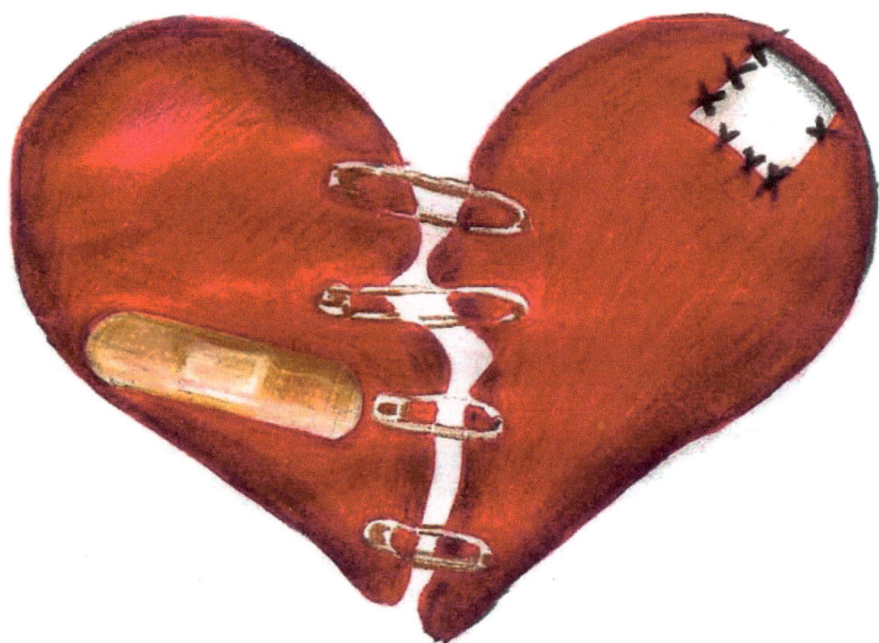

Welcome to Heartbreak

Perfectly still…,
Heart stood frozen in an unfamiliar dessert;
Dry breeze ruffled the air
But the brown dust stayed undisturbed in their sleep.
There was nothing in sight;
No trees, no flowers, no birds; not even bees
Beauty itself had denied its sight.
No tender look crossed its path;
Much less the pleasantry of a smile
It felt so lonely and out of place
That tears burnt its acrid face.
Lost and confused…it felt shattered with no hope of
being mended,
where did all this come from? It questioned,
how did I get here, just what wrong could I have possibly
done?
Streams drown themselves in its rivers
And rivers commit suicide in the seas of its sordid emotion,
In the mean time…,
Life and time kept sailing in their companionable boat
Ironically, as they neared the shores, the sea seemed to only get deeper,
Bewildered, life turned to time and question
'what manner of distress is this?'
'Life,' time sighed, 'welcome to heartbreak!'

The Inspiration to Write

The thoughts of a child are simply intriguing. I thought about so many things in my childhood years that it was impossible to keep all of it in my head. Since I was never one to speak much, I had to find an outlet for the questions and musings that went on in my mind. That is when I came up with the brilliant idea of introducing pen to paper. Sometimes, the words did not sound so good together and the lines looked more like a river overflowing its banks but I kept telling myself 'this is MY poem and it doesn't matter if anyone else likes it, it is MINE!'. So I keep writing. And of course there were always my teachers and very good friends to overwhelm with the task of reading them and telling me 'if they sound good'. With all certainty, if I could not find Mr. Leighton Elliott, I had to find Mrs. Janice Julal, Ms. Nadine Morgan or somebody from the English Department to tell me what to change and what they think about something that I just wrote.

While I value the input of my Denbigh High School family, I couldn't leave my friends out of the equation so Mettia Chambers, Marcia Williams, Dawn Bryan, Maschell Edwards, Ashton Johnson and Mar-Hugh Thomas, thank you for tolerating me and being honest when 'it didn't sound as good as the last one'.

I often hear that old habits die hard and that they tend to follow you everywhere and unashamedly, I have to admit that leaving high school and going to college, I maintained the same old tactics…Write, find a lecturer to share it with, share it with friends – anybody who will read! Las amorables chicas (Talsia Williams, Mellisha Ricketts, Shallimar Reynolds, Shaunette Perry, Kaydian Grey and Shana-Gaye Benjamin) thank you for always making time to read, critique and give me new ideas. Sharing with you was a joy. It was a thrill watching the faces of everyone who stopped to read what I write, the names are too much to mention on this single sheet of paper but it is their love that caused me to 'write the other one'. I am grateful for that.

I didn't know where the road would take me but I knew that I had found something that I really love. Making a step in the direction of such passion was the best thing that I could have ever done. It must be true then, that when you pursue your bliss – life will open doors where there had only been walls.

Secrets to Survival:
Thoughts for a cognizant you

- ❖ Excitement is like perfume; when sprayed, everyone catches its scent.
- ❖ If you enjoy your own company, I am very likely to enjoy it too.
- ❖ Success can be a painful experience; one must always try to prove that there is enough for everyone.
- ❖ Love is a choice to accept the faults with the perks.
- ❖ Words have the power to do what money can never achieve.
- ❖ True wealth is a heart full of love, a mind full of peace and a life lived with compassion.
- ❖ To know your friends, spend more time with yourself.
- ❖ Material things fill physical spaces but love and contentment fills the soul.
- ❖ When trouble comes we must be ready to stand alone.
- ❖ Words were used to create the world; use yours wisely.
- ❖ You own your mind; think something positive about yourself.
- ❖ Things happen, but so does consequences.

– *M. Pryce*

www.ingramcontent.com/pod-product-compliance
Lightning Source LLC
Chambersburg PA
CBHW042128080426
42735CB00001B/6